Good Grief
a collection of poetry

☙

by Stevie Edwards

Write Bloody Publishing
America's Independent Press

LA, CA

WRITEBLOODY.COM

Copyright © Stevie Edwards 2024. 2nd edition.

No part of this book may be used or performed without written consent from the author, if living, except for critical articles or reviews.

Edwards, Stevie.
Copyright © 2012. 1st edition.
ISBN: 978-1-935904-50-2

Interior Layout by Lea C. Deschenes
Cover Designed by Nik Ewing
Proofread by Jennifer Roach and Sarah Kay
Edited by Jamie Garbacik, Courtney Olsen, Alexis Davis, Sarah Kay, Gabrielle Dunkley and Derrick Brown
Type set in Bergamo from www.theleagueofmoveabletype.com

Printed in Tennessee, USA

Write Bloody Publishing
LA , CA
Support Independent Presses
writebloody.com

To contact the author, send an email to writebloody@gmail.com

FOR AMY

★

A prophet is not without honour, but in his own country, and among his own kin, and in his own house.
— Mark 6:4

GOOD GRIEF

Preface

When I was eight the doctor said the only way to fix my pigeon-toes was to break my legs and reset them straight. Dad said it'd be less painful to just let me walk crooked. And so it is.

GOOD GRIEF

Preface 11

For My Brother on His Sixteenth Birthday 17

What I Mean By *Ruin* Is… 18

Sunday Morning Pastoral 19

The Hippie Church I Was Raised in Doesn't Believe in Sin 20

Caesura 21

Wanted: Mummy Sleeping Bag 22

Meditations at Belmont Harbor 23

Enough Light to Harbor 24

Dysecdysis 25

Don't Call This Tenderness 26

Advice for the Manic 27

What's Needed 28

Hereditary 29

How I Came to be Built Without a Doorway 30

Apparition: Devil Child 31

For an Uncle I Know Only Through Letters and Collect Calls 32

Vespers: For the God of Breathing 34

Sweet Fifteen 36

This Is Not a Poem About Grace 37

For a Detroit Artist I Suspect
Isn't Really Named Mario Allegretti 39

I Want to Tell You:	41
Rising	42
Because I Could Not Belly Death	44
Say She Can Stay Veil to Me	45
Say You Were Never Sixteen	46
How We Failed Sixth Period Child Development	47
I Go Back to a House Party in 1979	48
Two Trailer Park Girls Go 'Round the Outside	49
Mending/Poem for Seth Walsh	51
Bacon & Butter	52
When Calling Home to Tell Your Dad About the Good Job	53
Glass Night Blessing	54
Let's Write a New Myth	55
ISO Chicago Accent, Smoker's Cough	57
Garden Apartment	58
A Photographer with a BA Joins the Army	59
Instructions for Grieving	61
What Remains	62
What I Can Say I've Left, What I've Mourned	63
Aporia	64
For My Brother on His Seventeenth Birthday	66
The Problem with Describing Winter	67

I Know No Ceremony 68
Disown 69
Because I Can't Take You with Me 70
Three Rachels 71
Thanks 75
Acknowledgements 77
About the Author 79

For My Brother on His Sixteenth Birthday

I am burning my brother on a rooftop
    in September. He doesn't protest much,
never screams. I tell him something had to give
    and it couldn't be me this time.

I tell him he's dust to me and sweep his ashes
    off the ledge. He keeps coming back
a boy and says it'll be okay. He points to the sky
    like something's there. I tell him it's gone.

I tell him anyone can be born—I was
    born yellowed by an unready liver.
He says it's his birthday, so I give him
    a beer and he pretends to like it.

He looks like he wants chocolate cake,
    so I give him another beer. He says
he's had enough, so I give him
    a cigarette. And he takes it.

He tells me he's cold. I tell him I held him
    as much as anyone could as a baby,
supported his needy neck in terror. He asks
    for chocolate cake. He points to the sky.

He tells me he's cold. I press my lighter
    to his sleeves and tell him it'll be
okay, hug him until we're both charred
    and warm. He tells me it's gone.

What I Mean By *Ruin* Is...

When there's only condiments left in the fridge
and you join a free online dating service
so men will buy you dinner.

When you've shucked the night with the dull blade
of indecision and gulped down everything,
even the pearls.

When some old, left-handed love has left
your guitar strung backwards
and you can't find any songs for rain
in its frets.

When you wake up next to the body
of your past and it looks ready
to wrinkle and bald.

When the last burn of summer is peeling
from your breasts and there's nothing to husk
the pale raw of new flesh.

When the woman who wears her hair in the old way
quits mumbling about Jesus on street corners
and takes her salvation pamphlets
to a pauper's grave.

When you're too ugly to pray,
but pray
               and the only voice
        on the drunk subway wails
                     good grief.

Sunday Morning Pastoral

When I say I woke up next to a cow this morning, I don't mean I woke up next to someone reminiscent of a cow. I don't mean someone who was just a piece of meat to me. I don't even eat meat, especially not in the morning, not on a Sunday. I mean—I woke up in a field. There was cow shit everywhere. I was relieved to find none in my hair. There was nothing sexual about this. I was not drinking last night. I didn't know what to do about how low the remains of the moon hung through the night. Something in the gravity of this May is pulling everything kiss-close to the ground. My body is heavy, pregnant with nothing worth naming. Sometimes fields are for eating in. Sometimes fields are for shitting in. Sometimes fields are for sleeping in. Cows understand this. My loves are still learning not to take it too personally when I prefer the company of mammals without vocabularies for guilt. The cows are teaching me about need. I don't need the armor of a suit of navy linen or the blister-bites of navy leather pumps. I don't need matching or shoes or excuses for standing still for five hours watching the wind lean the grass southward or for gravity bedding me down into a field or for smelling of shit. It's okay to be stagnant in my lazy filth. No one cares about the flies storming my ass if I don't. I can get used to the smell. Someday, I may miss something sweet in its pungency while catnapping on a subway ride to my cubicle. Nothing has been done that can't be undone with a loofah and lavender soap. Nothing worth how the night eats me.

The Hippie Church I Was Raised In Doesn't Believe in Sin

But I don't know what to do when my body becomes
furniture. The shelf of my back buried in crumbs
of infidelities we won't name. Steady
your beer on my shoulders. Would you like
some pastrami with that dry wry sulk?
Some mornings I bend into
a medicine cabinet, let you fill me
with what's needed to begin
your day. Some nights I splinter
your fingertips. *Don't give away
all the fine china on the first date*,
some noxious voice once told me.
I like to slide my saucers
under your door out of spite.
I've never turned into anything
I couldn't talk my way out of—
the Planned Parenthood receipts
my mother found, the missing bottles
of Vicodin and cooking wine.
I'm afraid of trying cocaine—
the police would find me,
a naked doormat welcoming drunks
to the subway entrance,
or they wouldn't, which is
exactly what loneliness means.

Caesura

I am extraordinary at getting on with
my day. The procession of debit card

swipes and Lean Cuisines. The ceremony
of accepting the bill for my poison, what ulcers

my nights. I think that maybe she would like
me to speak again, to find noise, to turn on

a radio, if there's a radio, if it's a decade ago
and there's a radio in the house and I still lip sync

the words to glittered songs about leaving, about not
settling, about leaving his clothes on the curb

before there's a *his*, before I've left or been
left. I don't think I can do any better

than to tap my foot to the rhythm of her
breathing. She is breathing. This is

good. Maybe I should tell her that hell
is not her body, not waking in a room

alone with it. What comes out is *preserve*,
which reminds me too much of shame

in the house—how she sucked the night
until it bled, how the night suckered her

broke as a joke. Maybe a joke would help:
a girl walks into a bar—no, a bar walks into

a girl and says *thud*. Sometimes laughter
is as impossible as praise songs.

Maybe I need to be still enough
to hear what wakes in her

and pounce on its neck, make it
screech, skin it alive if I have to.

Wanted: Mummy Sleeping Bag

I paid a woman to make my back more memorable and am left with an itchy swell that won't heal right. My body has spent a month protesting red dye. One friend says hydrocortisone cream and Benadryl. Another, to stop drinking and cut out wheat entirely, maybe survive off raw foods. I think I would like to stop. To hike into the quiet of cattails and rebuild muscles I've left in an unpaid gym membership. In the past six months I have paid four gynecologists to remind me there's nothing wrong with my body. I think I'd like to stop. I've recently discovered my sense of direction. I can find the quadrants of my apartment from the belly of any hangover. I want to prove I can find my way through April. I will set out early, wear less beautiful shoes than usual, pack an orange poncho from the dollar store, and walk until I don't recognize the sounds. I will need something better than a body to keep me warm at night, something weatherproof, snug as a wish for solitude.

Meditations at Belmont Harbor

A gory autumn absence.
This yacht coast alter I return to
like Easter Mass, praying
for a rabbit to pop out of the pulpit,
some new miracle worth watching for.
The sky's slipped into a new blue dress
and is lying about its age—
the full weight of the lake
crushing my pigeon chest.
All this, redress for loving him
whole: his lanky posture of grief,
gregarious grip of my hips,
matted morning hair, Jersey tongue.
I can't reconstitute the death dance
of staggering to bed alone into anything
like gliding: graceful swoop down
to the ground that is most mine.
What is most mine? Not love,
not the body rising. If I am to be
rolled from bed into daylight,
then I will be a black hole hoarding
every glittered dash of sun.

Enough Light to Harbor

> *Where is that sea, that once solved the whole loneliness of the Midwest?*
> — James Wright

The vacancy of atheist prayers and too much wine
walk me out to Montrose Harbor.

Dad said that in AA you don't have to accept God,
just that something is greater than yourself.

I press my palms together, tell the lake
I've always had trouble loving the whole

of a man, so I started with the dip in his shoulders
and ended with a strand of hair too dark to be mine.

I bought multivitamins today, which is the opposite
of killing myself. All my dreams are in French,

but I can't understand the sounds. I say
endless, something about light pollution

and gunshots, two hampers of dirty laundry
and no quarters, a guitar I can't play.

A man who looks too much like him, all beard
and bones and blue jeans, walks toward me,

then turns. I am the morning's torn lace
and aches, which will have to be enough.

If I walked into the lake, I don't think it'd leave.
The lake keeps licking the sand like I like,

which will have to be enough.

Dysecdysis

The raw morning of
troubled molting—
we say our eyes are cloudy
and ready, say good
riddance. We rough,
we slough and
slough our bodies,
lesions of tender
unskinned. The snake
doctor says this
incomplete shedding
is a symptom of
deeper illness. I can smell
my love making
coffee because this is
what love does
in the morning. *We are
nothing, incomplete,*
I wish into the scruff
of his beard, rub
his bald head for
luck or love. He
silently slices open
a melon, not quite
ripe but still
food—I take it
in my mouth. He
says this taking
without joy marks
the beast in me.
I rear my raw
neck back, ready
to strike like
the beast I am.

Don't Call This Tenderness

There's a shelter in your voice shaped
like a rustbelt factory, some gravel
I could kick into dust.

The air last night was thick remnants
of burnt coffee. We couldn't get its syrup
off our salty skins.

We were parched and trying
to suckle anything left wet
out of each other. We'd forgotten
about coldness.

I don't think you noticed the blisters
on my cracked heels
as you pinned them back
beneath your shoulders.

You weren't the first body to open me
against the damp dread
of summer sheets.

There's a man on a plane home from Jamaica
who's claimed the territory of my hip bones
with his lips, named them his
favorite part of a woman.

I'm not the desert type. I need
to see water to believe it's there.

Sometimes I get confused about the body,
go searching for its ends, ask the dark
skin of a barrel-chested stranger
if it's ever been mine.

Advice for the Manic

Sometimes in springtime, you'll want to fuck
the entire city. And the sun will say *yes*
to your doughy calves. And the cash register,
yes to a skirt too short for public transit.
And every raised mole on the bony back
of an old lover who said you were too much
sadness to levy will say *yes* this time, too.

And then you'll need a bigger city to strut in.
And then, an artist to peacock your back into
something stinging with joy. And then, a love
to peel the plastic wrap off and wash your tender
clean. And then you'll need more sensible
underwear, something pink, soft cotton
your mother could wash without comment.

And then, silence—invest in a solo tent
and backpack and other utilitarian items
at the Army–Navy store. Walk until you see
all the galaxies that have never touched you.
Summon ancestors who knew how to survive
the cold. Build a fire. Pretend you know how
to play harmonica. Pretend you hear crickets.

And then, return. The blisters on your feet
will heal into something tougher. Pay your rent
when it's due. Replace lost buttons. Never buy a gun,
even if you were raised by conspiracy theorists
and it's a bad neighborhood. Sometimes you won't
eat a meal for five days. Call this winter. Save
a little rum in your belly to unwolf into new mud.

What's Needed

A mattress needs to hold a soft body
without being jack-hammered into a hardwood
floor. A floor needs a body to sweep it for dead
skin and ashes. A body needs to breathe smoke,
maybe Marlboros or patchouli incense, to remember
an uncle finger-picking a 12-string, the strength
of GM-line-hands, what can be made of thin
steel strings and rosewood. A 12-string needs ears
to hear what's being done to it. What's being done
to it needs time. Time needs a mattress to collapse,
to forget what's been done to it. What's been done to it
needs a new dress, one with black lace. Black lace
needs a good fuck. A good fuck needs good
whiskey to burn away a litany of thou-shalt-nots
from a prudent tongue. A tongue needs ears
to hear what it's saying. What it's saying needs
sunglasses on an early-morning bus ride home.
A home needs a body to remember it. To remember
needs ritual: the good smoke, breakfast grease,
water and painkillers. Pain needs to remember.

Hereditary

There are loves who will kiss your thighs
and not wince at the decade-old haunts
of stretch marks. Remember your father
examining the faint red lines, devil's fingernails
on a chalkboard of pale skin, the sting
of ocean, a new bathing suit you'd saved
lunch money to buy. Find a man
who smokes too much and curses
without emotion. Let him hang you
from the bedpost, make your ribcage
his wind chime. Let him rattle you.
Open the window, pray for wind,
for anything but the summer sap stick
of air binding your bones to flesh
to bed sheets. Quit eating meat, don't renew
your food-stamps, eat only bread
until you find the visage of a virgin
on your dry rye toast. Remember the ache
of want in your father's voice the last time
he reminded you your mother was barely
100 pounds when they married.
Find a photo of yourself the last time
you weighed 100 pounds—
the shipwrecked eyes of an expired passport
staring out at what could become a double chin.
Middle school health videos warned
you'd lose your period. There's nothing holy
about blood. Praise the braveness
of collarbone, how ready your cheekbones
look to leave. Disregard your doctor's warnings.
Something is always going to kill you.
Your breasts will burn off last.

How I Came to be Built Without a Doorway

If a woman is a house, a shelter,
Mom must be only scaffolding—
so thin, her skin can barely
contain her bones.
Her mother's death,
a gaudy figurine
in every room she enters.
A man, a hypnotist, instructs her
to remember her origins.
She writhes against shag carpet,
mumbles about the dark
and wet, some unholy force
pushing her. Then cold air
everywhere. *I'm crying. Nobody
will hold me*, she repeats
and repeats until the man holds her.
And it will never be enough
to scrape her body off the floor
and tell her she's loved.

Apparition: Devil Child

I am a destroyer of necessary things.
I crush the garage door
into the butt of the Astro van—
a busted steel accordion.
As akimbo as an eight-year-old can stand,
I tell my mother that this time I am her mother,
that she should go to her room and wait
for her father to come home.
And she understands
that I have been the cancer cooing her life
into a gray winter bed
and will always be the Valium-head,
the vacuum, the vapor
who couldn't be bothered
by a knife lodged perpendicularly
in her young daughter's arm.
And she will always be stroking
my bald chemo head until it wears raw.
She tells me to stay dead
and slips into the comforting noise
of a sewing machine. She is
fashioning my favorite pink flowers
into a church dress. I know it's true
that I am as much her mother as she is mine,
so I stir furiously at cookie dough,
leave my sweet offerings on the counter
and pray for all her bad ghosts
to leave my body.

For an Uncle I Know Only Through Letters and Collect Calls

At fifteen, I edited Mom's letter
pleading for Governor Engler's
sense of mercy at the end
of his third and final term
to pardon you. I'm still searching
for the words to unload that barrel.
To bury guilt in the frozen ground outside
Calhoun County Correctional Facility.
To correct the way a belt with a tongue
for hymnals carved your back into
runaway statistics, into the beds
of semis, into the futility of collapsed
veins, into these prison bars striping
your face. To correct everything ether
could never shake off. The letter
itself was Mom's pardon for 1976:
for having to sit in a small town
Michigan high school, for the girl
(who I imagine had prettier curves
than Mom, less mousy hair, a face
not yet eaten by coke bottle rims)
presenting on current events—
presenting on two boys, bullets
for pupils, holding up the gas station,
a cashier bursting with a bouquet
of oozing roses. For the way
the weight of your sick guilt
flattened Mom into her desk.
And I'm told it was your buddy
holding the gun. And I'm told
you only got it to scare money
from a register into your dealer's
pocket. And sometimes I steal
things, glasses from low-lit bars
if my purse is big enough.

And sometimes I commit sins
of time travel, waking next to
strange backs. And sometimes
in the back of a van headed
anywhere, I cough regrets into
smoke. And sometimes I forget
your stuck-slow speech, your desert
eyes, all your fettered parts.

Vespers: For the God of Breathing

There's an *h* in ghost filling space
as in *hours* and *when*.

There's something tenant
in my lungs. Not ash—

don't shake your finger
at cigarettes I haven't smoked.

I've watched that choking death
before. Purple Lazy Boy next to

oxygen tank, hose hanging from
Grandma's nose. I held that veiny hand

as it let go. My clarinet waits
on warm, brown sound. I can't make

anything sing. Say if I hack up enough
green, I can buy a new pair of lungs.

 Say this pair grows only trees,
breath just catching in leaves.

Dad's chainsaw caught in a tree,
kicked back, hacked open his chest.

I wanted to lose my hand inside
the wound before stiches

closed him, to feel the raw of a man
built of rust and cold calls. Mom prays

in the name of whatever god or
HMO will have me, rakes religions

and pseudosciences for liturgies
to heal my chest. Perhaps some steam

and eucalyptus oil or repentance
can cure me. My life's been heated

by a wood stove and Dad's blood—
I can dab ash on my forehead whenever

I want. I don't need to give up
anything to be holy. Say I can evict

death. Say there's no space to fill
in *ghost*. Say you hear singing.

Sweet Fifteen

It is May. It is my birthday. I am shivering
on the bench in a piss-yellow softball jersey
as the sky spits a curse upon this year.
I am #2, which will never be my lucky number,
just the smallest uniform left unclaimed
by the slightly more coordinated
starting lineup. This will be my scrawniest
year, unless I live to be old enough
to watch myself shrink back into diapers.
I do not want to become the kind of old that needs
to be looked after. Some weekends I marinate
chicken breasts in lemon, oil, and herbs
to feed the awful, slow goodbye
of my grandmother's body. I will inherit
all of this dwindling. I am lucky
enough to get called up from the bench
and walked to first by a wild pitcher. I even steal
third. I have never been a fast thing. Nobody comes
to witness me clumsily catch a pop-fly, deep right field.
It is May. It is my birthday. I am shivering outside
the school, grass-stained uniform wadded
in duffel bag. Coach offers me her cellphone
to try home again. I tell her I'm sure someone
will come, not to wait late with me again.
And coach stays. And I apologize for my mother
again, as her gray minivan pulls up to transport me
home. And on the kitchen counter waits
a can of vanilla frosting and chocolate Jiffy cake mix.
It is May. It is my birthday. I am sliver thin.
I am baking myself a birthday cake. I will eat
my thick slice slowly. I have never been a fast thing.

This Is Not a Poem About Grace

The house is pregnant with something
unnamed. *But she was such a good baby*, Mom says.

The flies in Dad's throat have laid eggs—
that must be why the carcass of his voice
sounds infested by grief, if flies bring grief.

I don't know if this happens. I don't come
home. I don't know where to put myself
at night. I usually wake in Willie's bed.

I have this problem with lying. I don't tell him
my age. I like to watch the mirror
when we fuck on the bathroom counter—
he grabs my ass, calls this sexy.

When he tugs me close
by the belt loops to whisper, *I want
a child*, I do not remember how strong
my legs are, how many places there are to run.

He's out on the porch talking to a woman
from his home country. He weeps
when he thinks I'm asleep. He's from
a place my body cannot be.

I tell him I belong only to my flesh.
I weep for nowhere. I want to be
a waif. I'm working on being bony
enough to leave.

I don't tell him there's a room
with a bad bed in a separate city
where no man has ever slept.

I don't tell him my mom is turning
into a pillar looking over her shoulder
at the phone. I don't know
if this happens. I don't
come home.

For a Detroit Artist I Suspect Isn't Really Named Mario Allegretti

An overdose of stars squinting at Lake Michigan
detracted from the personals ad
etched in lines creasing your forehead:

> *30-something artist with a guilt complex*
> *shaped like Lolita, seeks*
> *late-teen girl, all sex and candy and cherry chapstick,*
> *a chip in her left shoulder too big*
> *to wrap a mouth around.*

We scavenged the wood line
for anything dry. You leaned
branches together into a teepee,
such a careful house for burning.

You jimmied the cork out with your pocketknife,
and we drank the best white wine
the gas station had to offer
from sandy paper cups.

The sky spat a baptism over
our entwined bodies. Afraid
of hypothermia and smaller gods,
you lugged me up too many dunes
to the vacant parking lot.

I awoke to snoring and wondered
at how my head had rested so long
in such a distinctly Italian mat
of graying chest hair.

You found me sitting cross-legged
in front of the easel, studying
your angsty depiction of some Detroit factory
saying goodbye.

You asked me to pose for you,
but I didn't want any rust painted
over my smooth, pretty hinges.

I Want to Tell You:

That once, my brother (just a boy then) found me
on my knees in the cornfield behind the house—
cold April night storm, hail stinging me, voice howling
at what wasn't there. That when he found me, arms
carved open by restlessness, every atom aching
to decamp, I couldn't see his face through the thick
dark but heard a whimper. That his eyes must have salted
for my wounds. That he cloaked me with his raincoat,
knelt, listened for familiar clamor of distant freight
trains. That he used to come out with me to place
pilfered spoons on tracks. That we'd wait for whistles.
That if we stood too close, trains would stop, afraid
we'd jump out of this town. That we'd peel flat spoons
from tracks, burn thumbs bending them into bracelets—
metal could bend, could give, not brittle like bones.
That, therefore, he grabbed my hand to pray for God
to still me. That sometimes what's needed happens.

Rising

Forget all poems that begin near
winter solstice and end
anywhere else. Rock back

and forth, bathroom linoleum
hard on knees. There's no more
Vicodin left, no seconds. Remember

how he consumed all light, arms spread
open in the doorway, as you peeled through
suburban streets into Christmas Eve Mass

for a man who returned from death. Try
to keep this death wish from fluttering
furiously against your stomach

with wings you thought you lost
somewhere between I-95 and "Sinners
at the Hands of an Angry God."

And it's true he never
told you his method, only
that the psych ward was crowded

with holiday blues. Tell the toilet
your body is not holy enough
to rise from this collapse. But

rise anyways, wings stringing
from bottom lip. Another morning—
still winter, sky too dark to find

your shadow. Tell your mom
you're bent by the flu. Nurse the raw
badge of your stomach. Remember

how he returned from death
a torn scab you couldn't bear
to hold. Say this is what love does.

It's too early to call this failure
grace. Curse everything
that won't receive you.

Because I Could Not Belly Death

I wait. There is a charge—
the drooling pool of regret
stinks the morning into blue
flowered sheets and yes,
I am in it, rank breath
of a dog, a sore opened
bloody in my stomach.
Each bland soup spoonful
stings with life. I can't
rinse the revenants from
the gauzy summer blouse
of fifteen. It must be true
I was a slender goodbye
song. Who can write a song
about the living without
gazing at death? I have no
singing voice. Most days
I don't consider fifteen
years I tried to snuff out,
all that life—there's an art
to waking, to stopping
by the deli, to masticating
roast beef and bread.
Like everything, it feels
like hell to swallow
the glad jitter pills
prescribed to addle me
into bearable. I must terrify
love as it tracks me down
in this daily dirge.

Say She Can Stay Veil to Me

Father, the girl is a sheer sheet strung
above busted window, always facing
east, always morning.

Hush the sun. She's too thin
for such prodding light, Father. Please
don't say rot—no, not this
hot, clammy fight.

Say she's only drying. I can see
she's burning, no fading,
the sick pale, a shit sight.

I won't draw her open. I'm not that
kind of kind. I could pack her up
in a trunk. I could hold her
folds in these soft-wrought hands.

Father, you won't take her either,
for fuck's sake, her night shakes,
pavement prayers. She's unlatched—
stunk at the sill for years.

Say You Were Never Sixteen

There was no apartment
in Battle Creek, Michigan,
melancholy as its tenants,
minor league Yankees
whose English stumbled
over pick-up lines.

No Bud Lite bottle filled
with cigarette butts wobbling
on a leaning coffee table.

No second-string pitcher
pleading, *Baby, please
don't smoke. You too young*,
as he teasingly took a slow
drag, exhaling hard in your face.

You didn't command, *Give me
a motherfucking cigarette*. You didn't need
ten tries to work the child-proof lighter.

You didn't puke neon
for an hour alone after
spiking a blue raspberry Slurpee
with cheap vodka.

 There was no ceiling fan
whirling July air heavy
with *arroz con pollo*. No bedroom
crammed with air mattresses.

No Aventura love song
whining from a boom box. No
punched-to-shit door
to close.

How We Failed Sixth Period Child Development

Three men waved the Sunfire over
to the last neon-lit shoulder
before city road sped away into highway
and suburbs. *I wish I was that baby
daddy*, one man sang out
and swaggered toward us clutching
his crotch in his right hand,
as if we had enough sense to aim
for that loud target. The lowering
autumn dusk cloaked the stiff body
of a robotic doll in the backseat—
a wailing, sleepless assignment meant
to teach us not to have babies yet.
The only white girls to get a dark baby,
we joked the teacher must've known
about our futures in beauty shops
trying to learn to temper our children's
coiled hair. The men took our orders:
orange pop and vanilla vodka,
a pubescent screwdriver. We left
the baby to freeze in the car.
Bad mothers of our own bodies,
we said we weren't scared. We were
used to each other naked by then,
a full six months chasing not scared
around the umber of grown men's beds.
The motel room was nothing memorable—
two big beds, bolted TV, lingering
rank of cigarettes, no visible bugs.
The third man, the one with no girl,
darted from bed to bed, inspecting
what he could see of our pinned flesh,
tried to grasp handfuls of our smooth
shaved spindle legs, until our chosen
gallants batted his probing hands off
us liquor limp specimens of beauty.

I Go Back to a House Party in 1979
After Sharon Olds

I see her, my mother:
    thin face, doll body, cocktail dress (something
    pretty, soft lace and cotton, never polyester).
Her seamstress hands must have felt their way through
    an entire city of sale racks to find anything suitable
    to drape her skin in. A 4-inch pair of red dancing heels
        I'd like to borrow. She's wobbling
over a thimble of tequila. Her big eyes flirting

    with everything they glimpse. She tells a friend, a man
who will never get a name in this story, she thinks my father,
    the waiter who rents this beer can castle
    and could sell anyone their own smile for dinner,
        is cute. I want to tell the friend
    to stop, not to push her over the couch, an ugly brown
that doesn't show the cigarette burns. Legs in the air,

she looks up at my father for the first time and smiles
    with her whole body like when she dots Chanel No. 5 on her wrist
        and presses it to her nose. I want to tell her
    in ten years he'll say all his worst nights started with tequila:
        two flipped cars, a drunk tank, punched out kitchen walls.
I want to tell her newborns are ugly, even

your own. Bit nipples of barely-A breasts. Blood
    and more bleeding, and he won't know how to change
    a baby or come home at night. I want to
  tell her a sharp subway turn threw a child into my lap today.
        The darling looked up and said, *Mommy?*
    I knew he was wrong.

Two Trailer Park Girls Go 'Round the Outside
for Eminem

I was fifteen when *The Eminem Show* came out—
a brace-faced, Michigan-poor scarecrow
of angst that the universe kept shitting on.
I hoarded cooking wine and Sylvia Plath,
pierced my own bellybutton with a sewing needle.
I was old enough to be angry at the litany
of nice things in the world that weren't for me:
cars, college, Nikes, sit-down restaurants,
ballet lessons, vacations. You gave me an anthem
for being born into a life that comes complete
with a WIC application and carton Parliaments.
For practicing my alphabet at AA meetings
through the smoky depression of adults
bemoaning their childhoods and wondering
if and when it would be my turn to speak.
Me and my girls screeched your mantras
in the backs of lunch lines and bathroom stalls.
We shook our awkward, little white girls asses
mostly on beat. And for once, I didn't need
to convince anyone I lived in a real house,
that it was just next to the subsidized apartments
and trailer park, that we didn't even have
any rusting GM carcasses on the lawn,
that the occasional twilight pops at the corner
were fireworks because we had so much
to celebrate. I want to take you back to the day
I learned the neighborhood boys burned down
the park playground and there'd be no more
swinging. I think you would understand
why I climbed up too high into the thinning branches
of the tree out back and worried everyone.
I'm still distilling my childhood into discrete moments
of no lunch money and second-hand clothes.
Em—I hope it's okay if I call you that—

I think my mother did her best with what she had.
I'm a college graduate with food-stamps
and no furniture. Everything I own is fraying
and loved. Last night I slow danced
with a woman. When I lost step twirling,
she said I needed to learn to follow
a good lead. My wine-stained mouth slurred,
I just got confused because you let go of my hand.

Mending/Poem for Seth Walsh

I had the idea that the world's so full of pain
it must sometimes make a kind of singing.
— Robert Hass

Every day people wake with spines in need of mending, nights spent spooning absence. There's no sense in cursing at the barista for the chew of grounds in your latte. Sometimes it's impossible to get a job right, especially early mornings, especially when there's a frontier of people impatient to leave you. You've miscarried jobs before. A belayer, you made sure the man put his harness on snug, told him if his foot slipped off the fidgeting cable, you'd hold him flopping around in the treetops. One foot in front of the other, the stuck pulley, you should have noticed the slack was too much to save him, no point in the care you put into the knots. He didn't slip or sue you. Call this grace if you can believe in grace today. The news didn't say what kind of knot the boy tied. His parents found him with his freckles still on. It doesn't matter what kind of tree as long as the boughs were strong enough to bear him. Perhaps you could've moved to California and told him a faggot is a bundle of twigs, but who's to say he wasn't ready to set himself on fire? Or, you could've told him the kids meant he was a fancy stitch that binds delicate fabrics, old lace to silk, but it's hard to feel fancy while bees swarm your eyes. But sometimes the dictionary is useless, which is what you tell your dad when he says that in *Merriam Webster* it says marriage is between a man and a woman. And you don't mention too much gin grinding your body against your roommate's or the small of a younger woman's back in the morning but bring home a law-school-boy from a good family to plan your future over strawberry pie. The boy probably didn't drink coffee yet. He might have grown to make chewy lattes too slowly. Maybe he'd never learn to sew, hem his pants with staples. What must be true is this: if a boy hangs from a sturdy branch alone, if wind swings his limbs for hours, it makes a sound here.

Bacon & Butter

I was raised on the principle
that bacon & butter can make anything better.
I watched my two-job Dad grease groans from
his waking bones, growing wide as a penance
for his absence. I'd like to grow wide
as a field if it means I can lie down
in myself while sky waits
on sun to rise.

When Calling Home to Tell Your Dad About the Good Job
November 2, 2010

Say no more food-stamps, minimum credit card payments, unfilled prescriptions, terror in small failures (lost keys, broken glasses, library fines). Tell him as much safety as the middle class can afford.

Don't mistake his silence for apathy. Listen: a family of five raised on less than that, Friday and Saturday nights taxiing drunk Michigan State students, copier commission sales in a decade of car plants closing, food and a roof over your head.

This is not the time to say you raised his son more than he did, babysat and prepared dinner for a family of five as an eight-year-old, slept anywhere but his house as a teenager.

When he says congratulations, say thank you. When he adds that maybe you'll be less liberal now that you've got money to tax and isn't it great that his Republicans won today, don't say your non-profit job only exists because of federal grants.

He will probably boast to his co-workers the next day, especially to your ex-boyfriend's father, show them a photo of when you had longer hair and a thinner face, and say something about good raising.

Tell him you earned it. Worked your ass off as their intern. The earn is more important than the it. Say you'll come home: Thanksgiving and Christmas. Say paid holidays and enough money for train fare. Say enough. Say thank you. Then say it again.

Glass Night Blessing

A boy, a half-decade too young, brings me roses
at work, like I'm a woman who owns a vase.
I fixed the snapped silver clasp of my favorite
necklace tonight, the one I snagged off,
too drunk for the precision of fingers.
When I was a child church ladies said
I had piano fingers, so I prayed for a piano
so hard I found music in every empty space.
I sang praise from my snug closet walls
and the branches of the cherry tree out back.
I never shut up. Mom would leave me
in the bath alone. She knew I wasn't drowning.
I never shut up. It took me years to understand
I came from a lineage of tone-deaf housewives.
But I bent the forgiving metal of this clasp
between slender thumb and middle finger
with such precision it must've made
a shattering pitch. Thank god there wasn't
any glass in the room. It's comforting to say
that everything happens for a reason.
I never got my piano. Nobody I've loved
has ever given me a rose when I loved them.
I didn't take the 63rd bus home from work
the night the boys threw bricks through
the windows near Cottage. When shards
must've had their two seconds of night glitter
before nicking a woman's hand. When the bus
evacuated into the street. When the boys
shot a another boy who evacuated that breaking.
I am this blessed: I don't know how to judge
if gun wounds in movies are realistic.

LET'S WRITE A NEW MYTH
for M

Some man cracked your mother's exoskeleton
despite her strength. You surfaced
from that raw in her belly and fed
off what you could find. The god of smoke
that smells of burning rubber hung her
through the night by the right ankle
above the constant take of Garfield Park.
Some weight (I suspect you know
better than I) snapped her last grasping limb.

Once, I watched my college roommate spray
a freshly hatched spider's nest with Aqua Net
to better the burning. She borrowed my lighter.
I didn't smoke often. The limbs ashed first.
I've never had the tenacity for saving things.
I don't want to leave you in the ashes
of a body that's burned from the lungs out.

I'll stop assigning any books that speak
of mothers. Let's read the tarantula book again.
Poison and *paralyze* are still too hard
to sound out, but we both know what it's like
to be unmovable—the way her death sunk
its fangs into your shoulders, the way
your shoulders sink into another detention.

Say you hate me again. Say I should go back
where all the white people go again.
But get off that desk—arms spread open
like the birds that don't fly here, like I could be
a nest for landing. Don't ask, *I can be
your big baby?* again. Don't jump
into my arms. They're too thin for cradling
a boy with bones turned stone by little girls
cackling in the backs of lunch lines about
another crack-head dead. I can't sell you
on any response sweeter than violence.

I worked retail for years. My hands are good
at folding things. I can fold you into
a picnic basket, send you downriver,
let the current take you where I won't.
I don't want to be the one to tell you
we're mammals. Let's write a new myth,
one without fire, that begins with live birth
and ends wherever you like. Sometimes
the news still airs stories about grace.

ISO Chicago Accent, Smoker's Cough

Sometimes Chicago says goodbye with a tire iron, a gallon of gasoline, and a promise, and I still want it to take me back. I like to dip my fingertips in the pooled wax of lit candles and peel the paraffin off. I like to have my hair pulled. I've never been hit by a man I wasn't related to. I only can walk like a lady in heels when I'm walking away. I feel relieved when fire trucks stop in front of apartments that aren't mine. I like the smell of tobacco when I'm trying to sleep. I was born with my grandmother's bad lungs. I can't chase anything down. Sometimes I try when I drink too much. I wake up bloody-kneed and alone. In college I won a prize for best kisser. I quit studying economics to write poetry. I know how to calculate the Gini coefficient of a hungry city but can't solve anything, not even dinner for one. On my last day in Chicago, I gave a homeless man a twenty and felt a little better. I'd like to give you a try, especially if you've quit at least one addiction and still shake out of habit at night. I'd like to feel a little better about my life. I curse worst in the morning. I'm not sure about love, but I'd like somebody to make me coffee, maybe bacon and eggs. I'll give you everything but a key to my place. I'll say your name until you wish you were never given it. Stranger, I can bend into anything but a wife.

Garden Apartment
for JPD

Before I moved into the garden apartment,
you'd already been living in its dread air
for the worst part of a year with another woman
who was impossibly messier than I am.
You weren't lovers. Neither were we.
Before the spent white wine bottles lined the kitchen,
before the molded bones in Popeye's chicken boxes
haunted the sink cupboard, there was a flood—
nothing dangerous, just burst pipes, damp
mattress on the floor, damp books,
a history of lovers that wouldn't dry out.
There were moments I considered buying flowers
for the plywood we called a kitchen table,
trying to sew drapes, scrubbing the black mold
off the bathroom floorboard. It's easier to live
out of boxes than to make any space feel
like a nightlight. In less transient cities,
a bedroom can say goodbye for months
before anyone listens. I think we listen
too hard. Before here, you were a father.
You are a father. I can't fathom the shape
of that absence. I am not very good
to live with. Once, I stole your frozen
chicken breast from the freezer to feed
the landlord's dog. You were in Ohio,
visiting your sons. I didn't own any meat.
The dog was too much hunger to ignore,
pitching his body against the fence.
I think I let it go too long, the flesh
stuck to the oiled pan, dry but not burnt.
The dog wouldn't stop licking the smell
off the plate, nibbled at my fingers
when I took it away to wash clean.

A Photographer with a BA Joins the Army

Because he fell in love with the word *unbearable*.
Because he loathed shooting portraits of wrinkled
baby heads. Because of drinking
bad Michigan wine in his parents' basement,
chanting *California, California,
California*—a restless prayer.
Can I blame him for having no magic
diamonding his dead carbon
drone? For years he's punched
everything in his body, called this
event of bruised kinetics *breaking*,
freaking himself into a windmill—
glory blades for limbs. God,
he could spin himself new—
I've seen it. When he said *Army*,
I didn't ask why. And there was silence
jumping out the car window,
jettisoned prayers. Nobody said
killing. Nobody said *combat*
licking his ear at night. Should I
mention it's Christmas and the man's
my chosen family? If I say this
never happened, then does it
not happen for the narrator
ogling this story? If I say
please? If I say it again with
quietude, a deep hush that
quivers like a body in a bath towel
rioting, no reveling, in the cold
ripe morning? If I don't speak?
Squad Designated Marksman, the steadiest
shot: he's learning to guide bullets into
targets a kilometer away. When I said
unbearable in the first line I meant
visualizing the targets as boys

with no shoes—I meant years of
Xanax and night terrors. There is
zero-order to this poem. Reader, please
zoom back to the car and say *blood*.

Instructions for Grieving
for Garth

It's best not to look at things that hang—
mobiles, swings, wrecking balls. Best not to
hypothesize how long it took the pendulum
of his body to come to stillness.

You can't be responsible for everyone's
happiness. Repeat this until it sounds
a little less like brake pads giving out
to these months of slush and ice.

Don't try to picture the room, how it must
have been gutted of light. Don't ask
what beam was strong enough to bear
his beer belly, what he climbed to get there.

You don't have to solve the way a body
refuses to become as simple as ash or even
balance your checkbook today. Just try
to hold the parts of you scattered.

The national deficit crisis won't mind
if you order takeout again tonight. Eat
and be whole. Don't let this death
thieve a room in your stomach.

Don't inspect your body for signs
of traitors. Your chapped hands couldn't
tie such a knot, crooked feet could never
kick the stool. Say you could never.

What Remains

A geriatric god wants me to feel this. Dread always begins in the joints. I rolled my ankle in the mud of Graceland Cemetery and tried to walk it off. It stayed.

What I Can Say I've Left, What I've Mourned

A full-sized mattress too soft for comfort,
springs sagging in the center. The empty
bottles of sleeping pills and Vicodin. I wished
like hell that bed would swallow my stinging bones.

The bed-bones of a man molded around a body
too soft in the center. A closet of sagging
church clothes. A belly that bottled the sting
of weeks without bread. A bleating prayer.

The empty of a bedroom with no closet
or bed. The hell of black mold swallowing
floorboards. I held a man's wish in my belly
for weeks until it bled, until it emptied.

A death wish I bred in my belly. The bread
of a church. I ached for years with that
body, that blood, pleaded for Vicodin
and a comforter that's never held a ghost.

Aporia

When the conservative lines
of a sleeveless funeral dress
shifted in the stick of July morning
to reveal a map needled
into my shoulders, a cartography
of home, my father asked why
I didn't love the body gifted me
by God, and by God, I believe
he meant himself.

Because it was his brother
in the casket and I can recognize a man
whose mouth has been hijacked
by the image of the liver
death he's campaigned against
with two decades of sobriety,
I said nothing.

I am tired of love that requires
beauty to come first.
There was nothing beautiful
to love about the embalmed
pudgy face of my uncle,
but his daughters still collapsed
into condolences. This is
how family is supposed to
break for each other.

My uncle has been buried
three months, and I've been
binging toward him.
Stillness is a dead bird.
I am trying to keep moving.
Today I bleached the life
from my hair, dyed the straw
a disappointing fade of blue.

My father loved my auburn locks
enough to curse at barbers
for shearing any more
than the frayed ends.
I am constructing a mote
out of ugly. I crush midnight
into my skull. I am my own
gilded God of pain.

Father, wasn't it you
who caught my slimy body
as I exited the folds
of my first home? Wasn't it
you who later said I should've
stayed there, too much
nastiness for any man to bear?

For My Brother
on His Seventeenth Birthday

Because our eldest brother held a pillow
over your face
to make you shut up; because I had to hide
the soft fruit of your skull
from his rage at how
you drowned the room with your bellyache,
and he is now
the wealthiest man I know—
I lock all my doors. I'm sorry
you will have to define love in terms of
what saves you,
an ugly heirloom I've gifted to you.
*

Brother, this is my prayer for you:
Be still still still still still—

The Problem with Describing Winter

is it's not really a butter knife carving
ridiculously at my reddened wrists

and I'm not really an hourglass
of daylight dwindling. But it is

lowering with all its gloomy
magic—I am getting ready

for the white cold mornings
cooing me back to bed. I fold

the night in half with whiskey
and let the lovesick middle go

pace in the shadow of a city
that won't take leave of me.

I Know No Ceremony

for Christmas Eve dinner
for one. Should I summon

my mother's sugar cookie recipe,
roll out the precise dough

of my childhood, cut it into
Santas and evergreens

to eat with Thai delivery
and the dregs of gifted wine?

Should I adopt a church
with a children's pageant

and off-key singing? Maybe
walk far into the deep cold

until I hear a voice like
God telling me to go back

home—kiss the scratched
wood floor for being mine

and there and covered
in my very own dust?

Disown

In *Home Alone*, the boy—later traumatized
by the burn of aftershave—repeats:
*I've made my family disappear, I've made
my family disappear*, with equal parts
horror and glee. This evening needs
the opposite of wine, something like
coffee but less fluid. The wine needs
a couch near a window, one with full sun
to spread itself warm and dripping
with light. I cast my limbs far
into the deep. The dripping needs
a bathroom towel or old newspapers.
The towel needs a good wash.
I have left too many good things
in gutted apartments, small specks
on roadmaps. The first word I learned
in Chicago was gentrification.
The first in Ithaca, antimacassar,
which shares no root with massacre,
which is an unearned hyperbole
for being alone. I am burrowing
deep into a glacier for the holidays.
I need the opposite of terror: slow
rattle of radiator and chamomile tea.
I change my phone again, move
across town and don't forward my mail—
ward off the possibility of Christmas
greetings. At the end of the body
is a skittering toward the warm,
soft center of grief. I am nearly gone.

Because I Can't Take You with Me

I'm leaving you in the living room hiding
behind the rocking chair I held you in.
We can read the dinosaur book again
if you promise not to fuss. I'm leaving you
in those threadbare Tommy jeans your gut
plops over, the ones that cost too much
to let go. I'm leaving you in the kitchen
cutting shortening into flour for a crust.
I'll hull too many berries, let the pie boil
over and smoke up the house. I'm leaving
you in the Chevy truck, amber aviators,
something bluesy on the cassette deck
as the sky gives up its courage to someplace
miles down the highway. I'm leaving
you in the junior high library bent
over a story we never thought we'd stop
writing, self-piercings and guitar strings
and everything we needed in the ash
of a stolen cigg. I'm leaving you at the bar
with a whiskey neat, make it a double,
enough cash for cab fare and tacos,
maybe some horchata to cool the burning
night in your stomach. I'm leaving you
at the table stripped to your boxer briefs
with a mouthful of dark rum, but just one,
just one this time. I'm leaving you
in your polyester batman costume
next to my crumpled cardboard crown,
our candy sorted and bartered for what
we think we want, before we know want
is a sin worth more than chocolates,
but less than staying here, less than this.

Three Rachels

★

Rachel #1 answers the phone when I'm trying to sleep and tells love to go fuck himself until he's sober, but love won't shut up. Love dries out in a jail cell. Love comes back to buy her a steak dinner. She says maybe I should give love a chance. I tell love to go fuck himself while I'm trying to sleep. Love comes back and builds a nest at the foot of my bed. I tell love I'm vegan, I'm celibate, I don't want anything I can't pluck from the earth with my own hands. I quit drinking, convinced rum is a magnet for the kind of love that needs an owner like a skeletal stray hound does. I tell love to get help, get well, shake his fleas at another doorstep. Love tells me to go fuck myself all the way to spinsterhood. And I try, And I try, until every subway car is full of porn stars who want to kiss my belly and tug my hair. And I can't get the salty promise of summer off my skin, so I slip into a bath of red wine and wait for love to come join me.

★

Rachel #2 says we have to be willing to be fools for love. When her worst love decided to go be worst for someone else who didn't mistake his bucking for gladness, she dyed her red hair blue with Kool-Aid. One fall before the cold took hold of the ground, we dazzled the quad with chalk rainbows, told passersby our love could be bigger than our fathers planned for us. She changed her last name this fall. I wasn't invited. Next love, I promise to be foolish. I'll spend my next month's rent tattooing your name somewhere visible. I'll scour the yellowing pages of my grandmother's cookbook, bake you a cake without occasion, let you lick the rich buttered batter from the beaters. I will love you full. I will love you like a milk-heavy breast loves the prefect, gaping mouth that relieves its ache in the morning.

★

Rachel #3 says to go with the one who loves you biblically. She says this for her daughters, not me. My mother says she didn't love my father for years of their marriage but does again somehow. My mother is not a Rachel but once forced all the jewelry from her first love down a garbage disposal and fished it back out. I played dress up with the mangled white gold, loose opals gleaming in my palms. I don't have a garbage disposal. Today, I put on earrings from the last love to buy me anything less disposable than dinner. They matched each other. That was the best I could manage. Rachel #3 keeps saying, *if it brings me to you*. If it brings me to you. If it brings me to you, Love, I will collect ornaments from all the suitors who think I need decoration. One Christmas, after too much eggnog, I will bump a blown-glass bulb from our first tree. Its quick, splintered light will cut our socked feet as we sweep. And this will not be the last time we nurse each others' wounds. I am not good with fragile things, but I swear I will love all that you unearth for me—your stinted roots, all the tender you've long buried.[1]

---

1 "Rachel #3" references Rachel McKibbens' "Last Love" poem.

Thanks

I would like to thank Rachel McKibbens, Matthew Ritger, Aricka Foreman, Benjamin Clark, Jon Williams, and Todd Anderson for being readers of this manuscript at its many stages in development.

Thank you to Marty McConnell and the rest of the Vox Ferus community for believing in my work and creating a space for it.

Thank you to Helena Mesa, Julie Stotz-Ghosh, and Danit Brown for being my first teachers of poetry and creative writing.

Thank you to Lyrae Van Clief-Stefanon, Joanie Mackowski, and Alice Fulton for bringing me to Cornell and challenging me to become a better writer.

Thank you to my Cornell friends, especially Daniel Peña for being the best neighbor in the world. Also, a special thanks to Emma Catherine Perry for existing.

Thank you to Captain Derrick Brown and Write Bloody for giving me the phenomenal opportunity to publish my first book.

Other beautiful people who helped make the poems in this little book happen:

Amy David, Andi Strickland, Angela Zito, Jamaal May, James Davis, John Vournakis, Kerry Flory, Kevin Kern, Kristiana Rae Colón, Lino Pretto, Maya Marhsall, Nate Olison, Raymond Bianchi, Ryan Essenmacher, Ruthie Spalding, Sarah Julian, Stacy Fox, Stephanie Lane Sutton, Stephen Pettinga, and Tristan Silverman.

Acknowledgements

Ampersand: "The Hippie Church I Was Raised in Doesn't Believe in Sin" and "Let's Write a New Myth"

Bestiary: "Sunday Morning Pastoral" (as "Lessons from Cows") and "Two Trailer Park Girls Go 'Round the Outside"

decomP: "Bacon & Butter"

The Desperate Reader: "Glass Night Blessing," and "ISO Chicago Accent, Smoker's Cough"

Fox Chase: "I Go Back to a House Party in 1979" and "What I Can Say I've Lost, What I've Mourned"

kill author: "Advice for the Manic," "Caesura," and "Instructions for Grieving"

The Legendary: "Say You Were Never Sixteen"

Mobius: "When Calling Home to Tell Your Dad About the Good Job"

Moon Milk Review: "Say She Can Stay Veil to Me"

Night Train: "For an Uncle I Know Only Through Letters and Collect Calls"

Orange Quarterly: "I Want to Tell You," "For My Brother on His Sixteenth Birthday," and "Three Rachels"

Radius: "Mending"

Rattle: "What I Mean by *Ruin* Is…"

Thieves Jargon: "What's Needed"

Union Station: "Hereditary" (as "Notes for a Cosmopolitan Woman")

Weave Magazine: "Dysecdysis"

Word Riot: "For a Detroit Artist I Suspect Isn't really Named Mario Allegretti"

About the Author

Dr. Stevie Edwards is an Assistant Professor at Clemson University and Poetry Editor of The South Carolina Review. Stevie's poems have appeared in Poetry, American Poetry Review, TriQuarterly, The Southern Review, and elsewhere. They are the author of Quiet Armor (Northwestern University Press, 2023), Sadness Workshop (Button Poetry, 2018), Humanly (Small Doggies Press, 2015), and Good Grief (Write Bloody Publishing, 2012). They hold a PhD from the University of North Texas and an MFA from Cornell University. Originally a Michigander, they now live in South Carolina with their husband and a small herd of rescue pitbulls.

New Write Bloody Books for 2024

Barely Amazing: Selected Poems (Shane Koyzcan)

An anthology of some of Shane's most requested poems on tour. This collection spans decades and includes works from many of his books.

Built by Storms (Miriam Kramer)

Miriam Kramer's *Built By Storms* explores the intricate interplay between grief and trauma, hope and recovery.

I Now Pronounce You (Caroline Earleywine)

What does it mean to love someone well? What does it mean to be a good daughter, or a good wife? What does it look like to step outside the way these roles have been prescribed to us?

Let Go with the Lights On (Lexi Pelle)

Through the lens of pop culture, these candid narratives reimagine beauty standards and grapple with the awkwardness of girlhood, struggles with body image and recovery, and questions of faith.

Wailing on Whisper Street (Bree Bailey)

The verses are rooted in the determined life of a Latina mother and fearlessly confront pervasive issues of sexism and femininity.

OTHER WRITE BLOODY BOOKS

Great Balls of Flowers
Steve Abee's poetry is accessible, insightful, hilarious, compelling,
upsetting, and inspiring. TNB Book of the Year.

Everything Is Everything
The latest collection from poet Cristin O'Keefe Aptowicz,
filled with crack squirrels, fat presidents, and el Chupacabra.

Working Class Represent
A young poet humorously balances an office job with the life
of a touring performance poet in Cristin O'Keefe Aptowicz's third book of poetry

Oh, Terrible Youth
Cristin O'Keefe Aptowicz's plump collection commiserates and celebrates
all the wonder, terror, banality and comedy that is the long journey to adulthood.

Hot Teen Slut
Cristin O'Keefe Aptowicz's second book recounts stories of
a virgin poet who spent a year writing for the porn business.

Dear Future Boyfriend
Cristin O'Keefe Aptowicz's debut collection of poetry tackles
love and heartbreak with no-nonsense honesty and wit.

38 Bar Blues
C. R. Avery's second book, loaded with bar-stool musicality and brass-knuckle
poetry.

Catacomb Confetti
Inspired by nameless Parisian skulls in the catacombs of France,
Catacomb Confetti assures Joshua Boyd's poetic immortality.

Born in the Year of the Butterfly Knife
The Derrick Brown poetry collection that birthed Write Bloody Publishing. Sincere,
twisted, and violently romantic.

I Love You Is Back
A poetry collection by Derrick Brown.
"One moment tender, funny, or romantic, the next, visceral, ironic,
and revelatory—Here is the full chaos of life." (Janet Fitch, *White Oleander*)

Scandalabra
Former paratrooper Derrick Brown releases a stunning collection of poems written at
sea and in Nashville, TN. About.com's book of the year for poetry.

Workin' Mime to Five
Dick Richards is a fired cruise ship pantomimist. You too can learn
his secret, creative pantomime moves. Humor by Derrick Brown.

Don't Smell the Floss
Award-winning writer Matty Byloos' first book of bizarre, absurd, and deliciously
perverse short stories puts your drunk uncle to shame.

Reasons to Leave the Slaughter
Ben Clark's book of poetry revels in youthful discovery from the heartland
and the balance between beauty and brutality.

Birthday Girl with Possum
Brendan Constantine's second book of poetry examines the invisible lines between wonder & disappointment, ecstasy & crime, savagery & innocence.

The Bones Below
National Slam Champion Sierra DeMulder performs and teaches with the release of her first book of hard-hitting, haunting poetry.

The Constant Velocity of Trains
The brain's left and right hemispheres collide in Lea Deschenes' Pushcart-Nominated book of poetry about physics, relationships, and life's balancing acts.

Heavy Lead Birdsong
Award-winning academic poet Ryler Dustin releases his most definitive collection of surreal love poetry.

Uncontrolled Experiments in Freedom
Boston underground art scene fixture Brian Ellis becomes one of America's foremost narrative poetry performers.

Yesterday Won't Goodbye
Boston gutter punk Brian Ellis releases his second book of poetry, filled with unbridled energy and vitality.

Write About an Empty Birdcage
Debut collection of poetry from Elaina M. Ellis that flirts with loss, reveres appetite, and unzips identity.

Ceremony for the Choking Ghost
Slam legend Karen Finneyfrock's second book of poems ventures into the humor and madness that surrounds familial loss.

Pole Dancing to Gospel Hymns
Andrea Gibson, a queer, award-winning poet who tours with Ani DiFranco, releases a book of haunting, bold, nothing-but-the-truth ma'am poetry.

These Are the Breaks
Essays from one of hip-hops deftest public intellectuals, Idris Goodwin

Bring Down the Chandeliers
Tara Hardy, a working-class queer survivor of incest, turns sex, trauma and forgiveness inside out in this collection of new poems.

City of Insomnia
Victor D. Infante's noir-like exploration of unsentimental truth and poetic exorcism.

The Last Time as We Are
A new collection of poems from Taylor Mali, the author of "What Teachers Make," the most forwarded poem in the world.

In Search of Midnight: the Mike Mcgee Handbook of Awesome
Slam's geek champion/class clown Mike McGee on his search for midnight through hilarious prose, poetry, anecdotes, and how-to lists.

1,000 Black Umbrellas
Daniel McGinn's first internationally released collection from 'everyone's favorite unknown author' sings from the guts with the old school power of poetry.

Over the Anvil We Stretch
2-time poetry slam champ Anis Mojgani's first collection: a Pushcart-Nominated batch of backwood poetics, Southern myth, and rich imagery.

The Feather Room
Anis Mojgani's second collection of poetry explores storytelling and poetic form while traveling farther down the path of magic realism.

Animal Ballistics
Trading addiction and grief for empowerment and humor with her poetry, Sarah Morgan does it best.

Rise of the Trust Fall
Award-winning feminist poet Mindy Nettifee releases her second book of funny, daring, gorgeous, accessible poems.

Love in a Time of Robot Apocalypse
Latino-American poet David Perez releases his first book of incisive, arresting, and end-of-the-world-as-we-know-it poetry.

No More Poems About the Moon
A pixilated, poetic and joyful view of a hyper-sexualized, wholeheartedly confused, weird, and wild America with Michael Roberts.

The New Clean
Jon Sands' poetry redefines what it means to laugh, cry, mop it up and start again.

Miles of Hallelujah
Slam poet/pop-culture enthusiast Rob "Ratpack Slim" Sturma shows first collection of quirky, fantastic, romantic poetry.

Sunset at the Temple of Olives
Paul Suntup's unforgettable voice merges subversive surrealism and vivid grief in this debut collection of poetry.

Spiking the Sucker Punch
Nerd heartthrob, award-winning artist and performance poet, Robbie Q. Telfer stabs your sensitive parts with his wit-dagger.

Racing Hummingbirds
Poet/performer Jeanann Verlee releases an award-winning book of expertly crafted, startlingly honest, skin-kicking poems.

Live for a Living
Acclaimed performance poet Buddy Wakefield releases his second collection about healing and charging into life face first.

Gentleman Practice
Righteous Babe Records artist and 3-time International Poetry Champ Buddy Wakefield spins a nonfiction tale of a relay race to the light.

How to Seduce a White Boy in Ten Easy Steps
Debut collection for feminist, biracial poet Laura Yes Yes dazzles with its explorations into the politics and metaphysics of identity.

WRITE BLOODY ANTHOLOGIES

The Elephant Engine High Dive Revival (2009)
Our largest tour anthology ever! Features unpublished work by
Buddy Wakefield, Derrick Brown, Anis Mojgani and Shira Erlichman!

The Good Things About America (2009)
American poets team up with illustrators to recognize the beauty and wonder in our
nation. Various authors. Edited by Kevin Staniec and Derrick Brown

Junkyard Ghost Revival (2008)
Tour anthology of poets, teaming up for a journey of the US in a small van.
Heart-charging, socially active verse.

*The Last American Valentine:
Illustrated Poems To Seduce And Destroy (2008)*
Acclaimed authors including Jack Hirschman, Beau Sia, Jeffrey McDaniel,
Michael McClure, Mindy Nettifee and more. 24 authors and 12 illustrators
team up for a collection of non-sappy love poetry. Edited by Derrick Brown

Learn Then Burn (2010)
Exciting classroom-ready anthology for introducing new writers
to the powerful world of poetry. Edited by Tim Stafford and Derrick Brown.

Learn Then Burn Teacher's Manual (2010)
Tim Stafford and Molly Meacham's turn key classroom-safe guide
to accompany *Learn Then Burn*: A modern poetry anthology for the classroom.

Knocking at the Door: Poems for Approaching the Other (2011)
An exciting compilation of diverse authors that explores the concept of the Other
from all angles. Innovative writing from emerging and established poets.

WWW.WRITEBLOODY.COM

Pull Your Books Up By Their Bootstraps

Write Bloody Publishing distributes and promotes great books of fiction, poetry and art every year. We are an independent press dedicated to quality literature and book design, with an office in L?, CA.

Our employees are authors and artists so we call ourselves a family. Our design team comes from all over America: modern painters, photographers and rock album designers create book covers we're proud to be judged by.

We publish and promote 8-12 tour-savvy authors per year. We are grass-roots, D.I.Y., bootstrap believers. Pull up a good book and join the family. Support independent authors, artists and presses.

Visit us online:

WRITEBLOODY.COM

www.ingramcontent.com/pod-product-compliance
Lightning Source LLC
Chambersburg PA
CBHW060503080526
44584CB00015B/1527